NEVER A DULL CARD

Personalize Your Greeting Cards
With Funny Messages

by
JOHN CARFI & CLIFF CARLE

CCC PUBLICATIONS
LOS ANGELES

Published by

CCC Publications
21630 Lassen St.
Chatsworth, CA 91311

Manufactured in the United States Of America

Cover © 1992 CCC Publications

Illustrations © 1992 John Carfi, Cliff Carle & CCC Publications

Cover by Steve Gray

Interior layout & production by Tim Bean/
DMC Publishing Group

ISBN: 0-918259-40-1

If your local U.S. bookstore is out of stock, copies of this book
may be obtained by mailing check or money order for $5.95 per
book (plus $2.50 to cover postage and handling) to: CCC
Publications; 21630 Lassen St.; Chatsworth, CA 91311.

Pre-publication Edition - 4/92
First Printing - October 1992

CONTENTS

<u>SUB-CATEGORIES</u> (for each chapter)

General
R-Rated
Insult / Practical Joke

INTRODUCTION

Isn't it lame when you get a card with a syrupy-sweet, factory-printed greeting that was simply SIGNED by the person who sent it?

With NEVER A DULL CARD every greeting card YOU send to friends and relatives will contain your own funny, PERSONALIZED message!

Never again will you have to search for days through rows upon rows of greeting cards trying to find the right one to fit "that special person." NEVER A DULL CARD gives you over 350 brand-spanking new humorous or clever greetings for ANY OCCASION to add to ANY CARD you select.

The messages in this book work best in cards with blank interiors -- but they also work as toppers to those goofy, boring, factory-inscribed messages. Or, if you're short on time and don't have the 3 - 4 days to spend at a card store, just fold a piece of blank paper in half and create your own card.

From now on, your holiday card writing time will be cut IN HALF! But most important, your friends and relatives will have a GOOD LAUGH and get the message that YOU CARE! (And you may even find you have enough extra time on your hands to go visit them.)

HOW TO
USE THIS BOOK

1. CHOOSE ANY GREETING CARD ...

It can be funny, serious, plain or even a piece of paper folded in half. You are now going to add *y o u r* "special message" (selected from this book) to whatever is already on the card.

2. TURN TO THE APPROPRIATE OCCASION IN THIS BOOK ...

(Birthday, Christmas, Mother's Day, Wedding, Etc.).

3. SELECT ONE OF THE THREE CATEGORIES ...

or "type" of message listed under each Occasion:

A. General

B. R-Rated

C. Insult / Practical Joke

Your choice will depend upon either the personality of the person you are sending the card to -- or the "tone" of the message you wish to convey.

NOTE: In many instances, messages in a Category can be used for more than that one particular Occasion, by simply making minor adjustments in the wording (e.g. most Birthday messages can be switched to Christmas messages or vice versa since they both involve the subject of giving presents.)

4. PERSONALIZE ...

if necessary, adapt the message to your purpose by changing or adding words or names (e.g. switching "brother" to "sister" if applicable) so that the receiver will feel the message was written *specifically for them*.

NOTE: Most messages are in two parts: SET-UP and PUNCH-LINE (these are usually separated in the book by the direction *"[OPPOSITE PAGE]"*. Write the "set-up" on the inside right hand page -- and the "punch-line" on the back of the card. Or, on opposite right and left hand page if you prefer. Or, if you create your own card -- on the front and inside right hand page (examples are shown throughout the book).

5. SEND THE CARD ...

a card which will give the receiver a good laugh and send the "message" that you made a special effort just for them!

Right Hand Page

Dear Jim:

Because you're special
to me, you deserve
more than just a card!

(You can keep
the envelope too.)

Love,
Wendy

Left Hand Page   Right Hand Page

To: Mike,

The purpose of this card
is to cheer you up,
to make you feel
happy and nice...

so I can ask you
if I can borrow
some money.

Sincerely,

Robert

(TO OLDER SISTER)

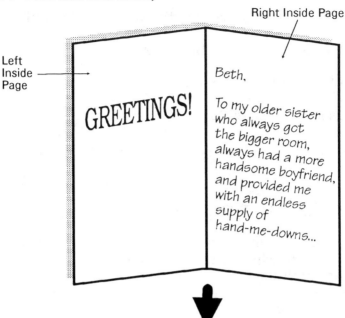

Right Inside Page

Left
Inside
Page

GREETINGS!

Beth,

To my older sister who always got the bigger room, always had a more handsome boyfriend, and provided me with an endless supply of hand-me-downs...

Outside
Back
Cover

Enjoy this small, ugly card I got at a second hand store!

Love,

Maryanne

Because you deserve only the very best, for you:

a 24-carat gold Mont Blanc pen ...

[OPPOSITE PAGE]

was used to write this card!

(WOMAN TO WOMAN)

A friendship like ours should last forever! There is no limit to what we can do with our will power! Our determination! and our <u>Mastercards</u>!

Sorry to hear you two broke up, but remember there are "plenty of fish in the sea!"
(Let's just hope the next one isn't another shark!)

(WOMAN TO WOMAN)

Guess what? I met the perfect man! He's handsome, witty and intelligent! He cares about my feelings, continually compliments me and tells me he loves me all the time!

(With any luck, I'll have the same dream tonight!)

(TO ROOMMATE)

As a friend, you give me companionship!

You give me advice!

You give me your understanding!

But most important of all,

you give me half the rent!

(TO DRINKING BUDDY)

You drank yourself into a stupor. You were blitzed for a week. You lost your wife -- your job -- your house. You crashed your car. You completely blew it. But somehow, you made it through the week -- finally sobered up, and now ...

[OPPOSITE PAGE]

It's <u>Miller Time</u>!

Tonight, I want to do to you what you've been trying to do almost every day of your life in shopping malls ...

[OPPOSITE PAGE]

get your clothes more than half-off!

(GIRLFRIEND TO GIRLFRIEND)

I understand you're having "men problems!"

[OPPOSITE PAGE]

Does that mean your prostate's acting up, you come too soon and fart in public?

First I'll take my blouse off. Then I'll unhitch my belt and let my dress slip to the floor. Next, I'll reach around behind my back and unsnap my bra and let it slide down my arms. Finally, I'll slip two fingers into each side of my panties and ease them down to my ankles!

(By the way, I hope you don't mind that I unwrapped your present for you!)

My dear Racheal:

I wanted to call you up and whisper dirty things to you, but my phone wasn't working properly -- so, I'm putting it into writing:

I want to sensuously rub your #*&@$%?!! Then lick your #&%@!! Then place my #%$&* between your $%#@?

Darn!
I'm really sorry -- must be a bad cardnection!!!

Paul

It is said that "with age comes wisdom!"

(So by now, you must be a genius!)

Regardless of what other people say...

[OPPOSITE PAGE]

I think you <u>are</u> worth the paper this card is printed on!

My Mother always told me that, even if you're angry with someone, you should always find something positive to say ...

[OPPOSITE PAGE]

GO TO HEAVEN!

I found the perfect card to match your personality!

(It was half-off.)

(WOMAN TO WOMAN)

Men! They're loyal, reliable and affectionate -- but,
then so is a dog, only they are easier to clean up
after!

Jane,

Interested in a tip
on how to look
beautiful around
the house?

Flip over all
your mirrors!

Betsy

[ATTACHED TO, OR WRITTEN ON THE OUTSIDE OF A SMALL GIFT-WRAPPED PACKAGE]

You know how shy I am. But enclosed are some of my deepest, most closely guarded secrets -- in fact, everything I ever wanted to say to you, but just couldn't find the <u>words</u> -- until now ...

[INSIDE PACKAGE: SMALL, POCKET DICTIONARY WITH A NOTE ATTACHED:]

And for convenience, they're all in alphabetical order!

(CARD WITH A BIZARRE OR LEWD PICTURE ON THE COVER)

Hi. Just thought I'd drop you a line ...

[OPPOSITE PAGE]

What's a nice girl like you doing with a card like this?

POORLY DRAWN
PICTURE OF
A FLOWER

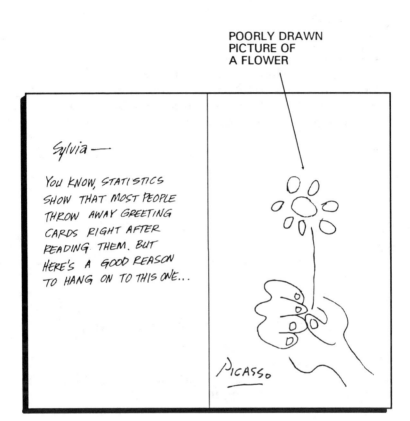

Sylvia—

You KNOW, STATISTICS
SHOW THAT MOST PEOPLE
THROW AWAY GREETING
CARDS RIGHT AFTER
READING THEM. BUT
HERE'S A GOOD REASON
TO HANG ON TO THIS ONE...

PICASSO

(WIFE TO HUSBAND)

Sweetheart--

From now on a five-course meal will always be ready for you when you get home from work! Your shirts will always be washed and ironed just the way you like them! Our house will always be spotless and the bed perfectly made up!

I promise you this -- but only if you promise me one thing:

[OPPOSITE PAGE]

to hire a maid!

(TO SPOUSE FROM A LARGE FAMILY)

Honey, I hope you don't take this wrong -- I think the world of your brothers and sisters -- but I definitely feel I got the pick of the litter!

The <u>second</u> happiest moment of my life was the **day** of our marriage! The <u>first</u> was the **night** of our honeymoon!

Happy Anniversary, Dear!

I was just thinking how lucky I am! Because, if you and I weren't together, think how silly I would look arguing with myself!

Happy Anniversary!

I can't believe you two are still together after all these years! I decided to look up the record in the Guiness book. Only one couple has been together longer -- and they're Siamese twins!

(50TH ANNIVERSARY)

Who would believe that you two have been <u>married</u> for 50 years!

(Most people don't even <u>live</u> that long!)

No privacy ... dirty clothes strewn around the house ... no sex ... screaming kids ... no money ... belching in public ... no nights out ... stupid, boring in-laws ... week-long fights ...

[OPPOSITE PAGE]

But <u>you</u> made it all worthwhile!

Happy Anniversary!

(OLDER MAN TO WIFE)

I may have had some sexual problems in the past, but you have to admit ...

[OPPOSITE PAGE]

I always kept a stiff upper lip!

I look at you two and see a couple who for years and years have weathered their marriage with grace, aplomb and savoir-fare!

[OPPOSITE PAGE]

Not bad for a couple of old farts!

(TO SPOUSE ON 50TH)

Happy 50th Anniversary!

Darling, to celebrate I'd like to dance all night long -- then have wild, passionate sex into the late morning hours! So be prepared:

[OPPOSITE PAGE]

you may have to jump-start my pacemaker a few times!

(HUSBAND TO WIFE)

Here's to my dear, sweet, <u>sexy</u> wife, who has given
me nothing but pleasure all these years ...

(not counting those five days out of each month.)

Honey,

*I love you because -
whether rain, snow
or dark of night...*

HAPPY
ANNIVERSARY!

*my MALE comes
everyday!*

*Love,
June*

Happy Anniversary, Honey! I love you because you gave up smoking for me and you gave up drinking for me!

(Now if you could just give up eating beans!)

Honey, I can't believe it -- each year you just get better looking! I wonder, is it your new diet? your new exercise program?? your new hairstyle??? Or is it time for me to get new glasses?????

They say "birds of a feather, flock together ..."

[OPPOSITE PAGE]

So how are you two cuckoos doing?

You know, you just keep looking <u>better</u> <u>and</u> <u>better</u> every year!

[OPPOSITE PAGE]

Well, I guess there's one advantage to having cataracts.

They say that couples who live together a long time begin to look alike!

(And you both look like crap!)

Honey --

Happy Birthday!

Happy Mother's Day!

Happy Anniversary!

Happy Valentine's Day!

Happy Thanksgiving!

Happy Halloween!

Merry Christmas!

Happy New Year's!

Happy Ground Hog's Day!

[SIGNATURE]

P.S. You know me and my memory, so pick the appropriate one!

Dear Wife,

Can you believe it? For the first time in years I didn't forget our Anniversary!

(Now if you could just remind me who I'm making this card out to???)

Congratulations on your new baby!

And I wish you many, many, many, many, many, many, many, many, many more! No wait! Cancel that. That's my birthday wish.

My hearty congratulations on the <u>arrival</u> of your new baby!

And my deepest condolences on the <u>departure</u> of your sex life!

(TO PREGNANT WOMAN)

Okay, your breasts are always sore and distended; you're growing excessive body hair; you have hormonal acne, saggy skin, stretch marks, varicose veins, swollen ankles. You throw up every morning and experience weird mood swings all day long -- and that's not even the half of it! But look at it on the bright side:

[OPPOSITE PAGE]

Whoops, I'm fresh out of bright side.

Now that you have a new baby ...

Your heart will be filled with <u>love</u>!

Your life will be filled with <u>joy</u>!

And your home will be filled with ...

[O P P O S I T E   P A G E]

<u>broken toys</u>!

———

(BABY OVERDUE)

I understand your baby is a little overdue!

(Have you tried, "Ally, Ally Out In Free!?")

———

You made it through nine months of pregnancy and suffering without a night life and without a sex life -- and finally your baby has arrived!

(So get ready for 21 more years of the same!)

I'm so happy to hear that you're expecting! You know, a lot of other women I know are also pregnant right now -- it must be something in the air!

(Like their legs!)

Congratulations on your pregnancy! Have you thought about names yet? Long ago, certain Indian tribes had a ritual of naming their children after the first thing they saw upon conception. Good thing we don't do that anymore or we might have names like "Kitchen Table" Smith, "Mirror-On-The-Ceiling" Jones, or "Whips & Chains" Johnson!

Hey, contrary to what most people say, babies are not all work. There is a fun part to having them ...

[OPPOSITE PAGE]

the conception.

Just think! You made it through nine months of pain in your stomach! But it's not over -- you'll go through the rest of your life with a pain in the butt!

He's bald, he has no teeth and he whines a lot -- but you love him anyway, don't you? After all, he is the father of your baby!

I hope your new baby looks a little like both of you ...

[OPPOSITE PAGE]

It'll keep anthropologists busy for years!

(TO A COUPLE WHO WAITED A LONG TIME)

There's only one thing harder to picture than you two having a baby ...

[OPPOSITE PAGE]

you two having sex.

Congratulations on your new baby! Hearing about all the trials and tribulations you two faced over the past nine months and how you struggled to rise above them has been a real inspiration for my husband and I!

(We've decided to get a dog!)

CONGRAT'S ON YOUR BABY!

Bob,

Welcome to the world of sleepless nights, drool-stains on your new shirts, diaper changing in crowded malls, constant worry about your child's welfare, no more going out to restaurants, no more going out, period. But hey, look at it on the bright side.....

....
....
....
....
...don't mind me, I'm still trying to think of a "bright side"..........................
....
....
....

Good Luck!

Jimbo

There is so much I wanted to say to you, but I just couldn't find the words ...

(So I used your birthday money to buy myself a dictionary!)

Hope you have an eudaemonistic birthday!

I was just thinking about what to get you for your birthday ...

A Mercedes? A mansion?? A million bucks???

(Like I said... <u>just</u> <u>thinking</u> -- but remember, it's the <u>thought</u> that counts!)

I can't believe it! Year after year you never seem to age. I wonder if you should see a doctor about it??? I think you might have contracted "Dick Clark Disease!"

You should never feel bad about getting older!

(The only other alternative is to die young!)

(TO 21-YEAR-OLD)

So, you just turned 21!

Congratulations!

This means you're no longer illegal!

Okay, so you're getting older. But look at the positive side ...

if you were a chair, you'd be a rare antique!!!

For your birthday I bought you a fabulous looking cake! But to be sure that you would like it, I decided to take an eensie-teensie, little bite. But I still wasn't sure, so I took another, then another. Finally, I was convinced! That was the most scrumptious cake and the most delicious frosting you ever <u>would</u> have tasted... Sorry!

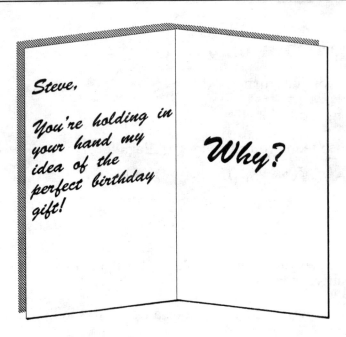

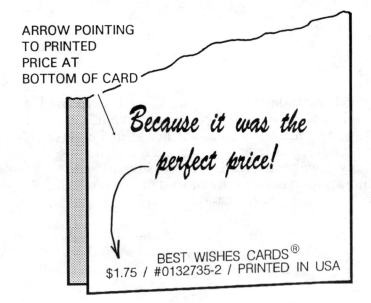

So, today is your birthday! Well, it's also National "Me First" Day. So, I'm going to celebrate by giving you this card and spending fifty bucks on myself!

There's something that comes around every year at just about the same time as your birthday ...

[OPPOSITE PAGE]

My urge to save money.

Hope you like the card.

I thought of a great way to celebrate this special occasion ...

We'll get a bunch of wild, loud people together. They'll bring balloons, streamers and a giant cake with your name on it. We'll stick candles into the cake and light them -- you'll blow them out while we all sing a merry song dedicated to you. Then we'll shower you with a whole bunch of wonderful, beautifully-wrapped presents -- you shake them, try to guess what's inside, then rip 'em op...

Nah! Too ridiculous! It'll never catch on.

For your birthday I'm going to make your dreams come true!

(Especially the one about a train going into a tunnel!)

Sweetheart, you remind me of a fine wine!

(You get better with age and I can't wait to pop your cork!)

(TO OLDER PERSON)

In many cultures around the world, elders are praised and highly revered -- but things are a little different here in America, so ...

[OPPOSITE PAGE]

Happy birthday you old fart!

(TO YOUNG WOMAN)

Happy Birthday and Congratulations! You have now reached the special age where you can be told the ancient secret of the two mysterious things about a woman that will surely lure a man:

[OPPOSITE PAGE]

" T and A "

(GIRLFRIEND TO GIRLFRIEND)

I must have gone to ten different stores today,
trying to find you the perfect gift -- but they don't
have a vibrator that respects you in the morning.

Happy Birthday anyway!

(ELDERLY WIFE TO ELDERLY HUSBAND)

You may be getting old and losing some of your
bodily functions, but you've got <u>one</u> <u>organ</u> that's
<u>right</u> <u>up</u> there ...

[OPPOSITE PAGE]

your brain!

(TO SOMEONE OVER 60)

You're getting older and I think before it's too late,
you should experience a <u>threesome</u> ...

Then again, at your age, a threesome is <u>mandatory</u>!

(<u>One person</u> to have sex with <u>you</u> -- and <u>another</u>
who knows CPR!)

*[NOTE: THIS MESSAGE CAN ALSO BE
USED AS A "RETIREMENT" CARD]*

(TO OLDER PERSON)

For this special day I had wanted to bring you a beautiful cake adorned with the traditional candles -- one for each year ...

(But the fire marshal wouldn't issue me a permit!)

In order to be successful and to get where you are today, you had to climb a lot of mountains! So on your birthday, it can truly be said, you're <u>over</u> the <u>hill</u>!

Worried about your age? Well, I just want to assure you, you're not getting older, you're getting ...

[OPPOSITE PAGE]

a LOT older!

Remember what they say ... "you're not getting older -- you're getting <u>wiser</u>." So ....

[OPPOSITE PAGE]

Happy Birthday Wise-ass!

(TO 30-YEAR-OLD) *

So, you just turned 30! Do you realize that's eleven thousand, nine hundred and fifty-seven days??? !!!

Now, I realize the purpose of a card like this is to convince you to stop worrying about your age ...

[OPPOSITE PAGE]

But how the hell can you with <u>those</u> kind of numbers!?!

* *[NOTE: 40 YEARS = 14,610 DAYS*

50 YEARS = 18,262 DAYS]

You're another year older, which means another year closer to senility!

(So I hope you don't forget I gave you this card!)

(TO SOMEONE WHO KEEPS THEIR AGE A SECRET)

Because you don't tell anyone how old you are, we never know how many candles to put on your cake.

So to be sure, this year we're just going to set the whole damn thing on fire!

I know you're getting older, but you don't look <u>half-bad</u>!

(Maybe it's because I have a glass eye?)

Here's a test to tell how to know when you're getting <u>old</u>!

First, look in the mirror.

Now, answer this question:

[OPPOSITE PAGE]

Do the wrinkles on your face outnumber the hairs on your head?

Good things come with age...

[OPPOSITE PAGE]

Unfortunately, so do hemorrhoids, gallstones and a weak bladder!

TAKE A <u>BLANK</u> CHECK AND PUT IT IN A
BIRTHDAY CARD WITH JUST THE
CORNER STICKING OUT:

THEN <u>GLUE</u> THE CARD HOPELESSLY
SHUT.

ATTACH A NOTE OR WRITE ON THE
FRONT OF THE CARD:

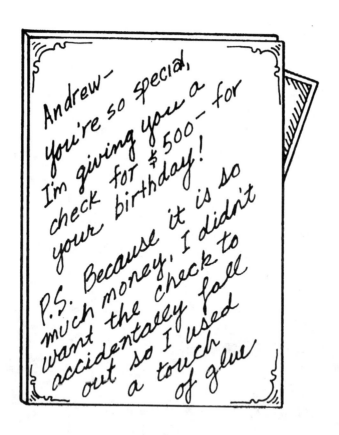

(ONE OLDER PERSON TO ANOTHER)

Frank,

Since we're both
getting older,
there's one thing
that's very
important not to
forget...Since
we're both getting
older, there's
one thing that's
very important
not to
forget...Since we're
both
getting older
there's one thing
that's very
important not to
forget...

Thank God I remembered your birthday this year!
My memory is not as good as it use to be -- so to be
on the safe side:

Happy Birthday! (7-22-93) *

Happy Birthday! (7-22-94)

Happy Birthday! (7-22-95)

Happy Birthday! (7-22-96)

Happy Birthday! (7-22-97)

Happy Birthday! (7-22-98)

Happy Birthday! (7-22-99)

[ETC.]

* *[SUBSTITUTE THE APPROPRIATE
BIRTH DATE]*

[ON FRONT OF CARD]

If you're like me, you like a birthday that is filled
with surprises ...

[INSIDE]

Surprise ... no money!

(TO A FIXER-UPPER DAD, UNCLE, ETC.)

*[WRAP A BOX OF CAKE MIX,
FROSTING, AND THE APPROPRIATE
NUMBER OF CANDLES]*

[ATTACH CARD OR NOTE]:

Because you are so good with your hands, I thought
you would enjoy this "Do-It-Yourself Birthday Kit!"

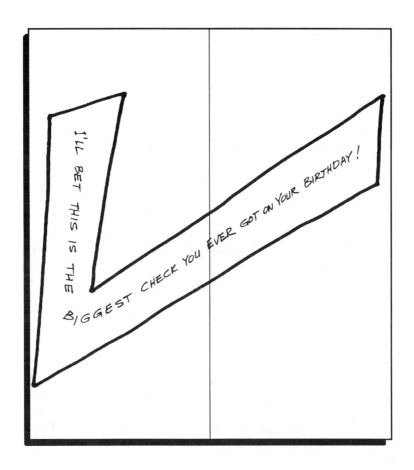

Sorry I forgot your birthday. And sorry I forgot to get you a present. But I have a perfect excuse why I forgot -- only I forget what it is???

Sorry I forgot your birthday, but I could have sworn you had one just last year???

I forgot your birthday and I feel so bad! There's only one thing that could make me feel worse -- if you didn't notice that I forgot!

Do you ever get that nagging feeling that you forgot something, but can't think of what it is?

Well, I seem to get it twice a year -- on April 15th and your birth date!

That's right, I'm late for your birthday this year --
and I probably won't be on time next year either,
because I don't own a watch.

But it's my birthday soon and some nice, thoughtful
person might want to get me one ...

Once again I forgot your birthday, but unlike all
those other times, this year I have a perfectly good
excuse ...

[OPPOSITE PAGE]

My calendar broke!

Because I like to be different, I thought I'd wait
until all the celebrating and hoopla was over before
I sent you this card. This way it would stand out.

Sorry I'm late for your birthday!

For a gift, I was getting ready to give you <u>myself naked</u> -- but the bow kept slipping off!

The reason I forgot your birthday?

Well, let's just say it concerns sex ...

[OPPOSITE PAGE]

I <u>screwed</u> up!

(GIRL TO GUY)

Sorry this card is <u>late</u> for your birthday, but my mind was preoccupied ...

[OPPOSITE PAGE]

Something <u>else</u> is late, too!!!

BELATED BIRTHDAY   Insult

Happy Birthday! Bet you thought I forgot! I really <u>did</u> know that it was your birthday last week -- I just didn't want to remind you that you're getting older.

Believe me, forgetting your birthday was an accident!

(But from what I've heard, so were you!)

Besides your birthday, there's three things I can never remember:

1. your color preference

2. what size you take, or

3. how to spend more than a buck.

I didn't actually forget your birthday -- you just had it too soon!

[OPPOSITE PAGE]

Which reminds me of your sex problem ...

[PUT YOUR NAME ON THE OUTSIDE OF THE ENVELOPE ONLY]

[INSIDE CARD]:

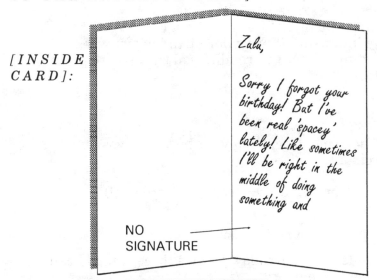

Zulu,

Sorry I forgot your birthday! But I've been real 'spacey' lately! Like sometimes I'll be right in the middle of doing something and

NO
SIGNATURE

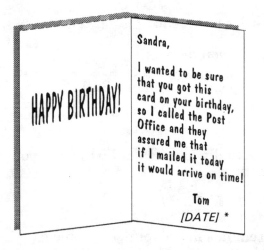

HAPPY BIRTHDAY!

Sandra,

I wanted to be sure that you got this card on your birthday, so I called the Post Office and they assured me that if I mailed it today it would arrive on time!

Tom
[DATE] *

*<u>TWO</u> DAYS BEFORE THE PERSON'S BIRTHDAY, BUT MAKE THE YEAR SOMETHING LIKE <u>1962</u>]

(ESPECIALLY TO A TEACHER OR A STUDENT)

Dear Ms. Chase:

I'm sorry I forgot your birthday
and I won't let it happen again!
I'm sorry I forgot your birthday
and I won't let it happen again!
I'm sorry I forgot your birthday
and I won't let it happen again!
I'm sorry I forgot your birthday
and I won't let it happen again!
I'm sorry I forgot your birthday
and I won't let it happen again!
I'm sorry I forgot your birthday
and I won't let it happen again!
I'm sorry I forgot your birthday
and I won't let it happen again!

I'm sorry I forgot your birthday
and I won't let it happen again!
I'm sorry I forgot your birthday
and I won't let it happen again!
I'm sorry I forgot your birthday
and I won't let it happen again!
I'm sorry I forgot your birthday
and I won't let it happen again!
I'm sorry I forgot your birthday
and I won't let it happen again!
I'm sorry I forgot your birthday
and I won't let it happen again!
I'm sorry I forgot your birthday
and I won't let it happen again!

(RELIGION UNKNOWN)

Here's wishing you a Merry Christmas and a Happy New Year!

And if you're Jewish -- Cheery Chanukkah!

And if you're Atheist -- Happy Nothingness!

(WIFE TO HUSBAND)

This Christmas, I wanted to give you something that would bring you hours and hours of intense pleasure!

(Unfortunately, my mother couldn't make it this year.)

(TO ANOTHER FAMILY MEMBER)

I was thinking back this morning, remembering how we used to sit around the Christmas tree, singing carols while we wrapped the presents ...

Anyway, it got me wondering -- do you suppose that's where they got <u>Wrap</u> Music?

This is the special Christmas season,
Which gives us all a special reason,
To buy those gifts,
Small and large,
And put them all on MasterCharge!

Now, I can't pen verse like The Bard,
So please accept this humble card,
And the "<u>thought</u>"
That's in it,
Cuz I am 3000 dollars over my limit!

I asked myself, as I was shopping today, "what do
you give the man who has everything?" Well,
Abercrombie & Fitch were fresh out of
turbo-powered toothpicks and remote control
toenail clippers, so you'll just have to settle for this
card.

*Happy Christmas
and a
Merry New Year*

-- from your ~~twisted~~ friend!

At first I was going to enclose a check for $100. But then I thought it over and decided just to give you this card. I suspect you're probably disappointed -- but at least this proves I'm not trying to <u>buy</u> your friendship!

Remember when you believed in Santa and got all those great toys every year?

Wasn't it fun to eat as much candy and cookies as you wanted -- and stay up till all hours of the night -- and still feel great?

Ain't it a bitch being a Grownup?

Enjoy this wonderful holiday, but be careful you don't overdo the Christmas "spirits" and then try to drive home ...

(or you just might become a <u>spirit</u> yourself!)

Honey, you know that list of Santa's and how he's going to be nice to those who've been good?

Well, this year I'm going to be extra nice to you -- cuz I like how you've been <u>bad</u>!

You'll notice there's no present with this card. That's because you'll get what I'm giving you <u>later</u> tonight, <u>in</u> <u>bed</u>!!!

[OPPOSITE PAGE]

It's kinda like the "<u>lay</u>-away" plan!

---

1. The outdoor lights ...

2. The tree and ornaments ...

3. Your panties ...

[OPPOSITE PAGE]

Name three things that are going to come down right after Xmas!

They say, "You have to take the <u>bad</u> with the good ..."

[OPPOSITE PAGE]

Like when <u>In-Laws</u> arrive with presents!

(TO LAWYER, AGENT, HIGH-LEVEL BUSINESS EXECUTIVE, ETC.)

I know it is considered <u>de rigueur</u> to tailor the present to the person, but I went to every pet shop in town and they were all out of pit bulls!

When I care for someone, I only give the very best!

[OPPOSITE PAGE]

You'll get your Ginsu knife in about ten days, along with your Chia Pet.

[OUTSIDE OF CARD]

I wanted to give you a special, out-of-the-ordinary gift this Christmas ...

[INSIDE CARD: A VERY OLD, BEAT-UP, DOLLAR BILL]

so I'm giving you a dollar bill that has probably traveled the world and helped thousands of people purchase millions of dollars worth of stuff ... can you stand the excitement?!

(TO OLDER PERSON)

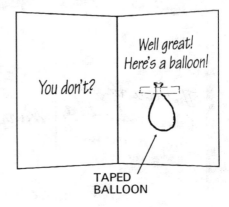

TAPED
BALLOON

[IF YOU HAVE ANY OLD CHRISTMAS CARDS SENT TO YOU FROM LAST YEAR THAT YOU DIDN'T THROW OUT -- ESPECIALLY ONE FROM THE PERSON YOU'RE WRITING TO, WITH THEIR SIGNATURE ON IT --WRITE THE FOLLOWING MESSAGE UNDER THEIR SIGNATURE:]

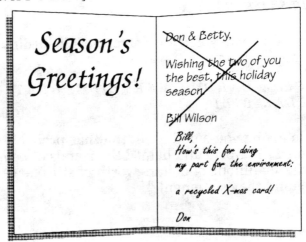

Dear Jan,
I've written over
200 cards and
I'm so tired I
could just
drop dea

CONGRATULATIONS   General

You <u>deserve</u> only the best!

[OPPOSITE PAGE]

But the question is, what will you <u>settle</u> for?

(WEIGHT LOSS)

I'm happy to hear that you <u>lost</u> some weight!

And I'm angry that it was <u>found</u> on my thighs!

(GENERIC)

It is not everyday that a person deserves to be honored for such determination, perseverance and genius!

[OPPOSITE PAGE]

But enough about <u>ME</u> !

-- congratulations on your new job. *

*[NOTE: WITH MINOR REWRITE, THIS
MESSAGE WILL WORK FOR ALMOST
ANY OCCASION OR SITUATION:]*

But enough about <u>ME</u>!

-- congratulations on your .... graduation.
.... promotion.
.... engagement.
.... retirement.
.... wedding.

-- congratulations on turning .... 40.
.... 50.

-- congratulations on finding the right .. home
.... your new car.

ETC.

Congratulations! Way to go! What a guy! You're the best of the best! You're superb! No one does it like you! Kudos to you! What a star! You're tops! Yes, it's true, no one can match you when it comes to really ...

[OPPOSITE PAGE]

loud farts!

Congratulations! You were superb!

You really deserve something special, but I'm not sure how to reward you, so I'm going to leave it open ...

(my bedroom door, that is!)

CONGRATULATIONS Insult

Congratulations! I hear you have finally found the person of your <u>dreams</u>!

(So who's it this time? Freddy Kruger!)

You're amazing! You're unbelievable! You're spectacular! You're the best at what you do!

There's just one thing that confuses me ...

What the hell do you do???

I'm truly sorry! I really wanted to be there in person to <u>shake</u> <u>your</u> <u>hand</u>.

(But I haven't had my shots!)

CARD IS
ATTACHED
TO A
PHONE BOOK

CRUDELY
DRAWN
CHECK

YOUR
NAME

(FROM A DRINKING BUDDY)

Congratulations! I cannot think of a more perfect couple!

(Unless it were a couple of beers!)

They say that <u>two</u> can live for the price of <u>one</u> ...

(But if you do the math, you're still better off living alone: <u>half-price</u>!)

Believe me, I wish you all the happiness in the world!

But I wouldn't feel right if I didn't warn you about the #1 thing that leads to divorce ...

[OPPOSITE PAGE]

marriage.

Diane & Peter,

Congratulations on
your engagement!

-Leslie

P.S. You know, I
really shouldn't have
to say that because
I'm sure you two
have been _engaging_
long before this.

LUCKY
YOU!

(GIRLFRIEND TO GIRLFRIEND)

Hey, you're getting married! Just think of all the
excitement that awaits you: Incredible sex on table
tops! In the shower! Hanging from the chandelier!

(And then, when your husband gets home from
work, you get to do it all over again!)

(TO CO-WORKER)

So, he finally proposed? Bet you thought it would never happen, eh? So did most of us here at the office. Well, I want you to know I am really happy for you. But I'd be a lot happier if he would have waited about six more months -- cuz then I would have won the office pool.

[SIGNATURE]

P.S. I had one of the <u>low</u> numbers!

(TO SOMEONE MARRYING A DIVORCEE)

Congratulations on your engagement!

I hope you have a very happy life -- I realize your husband's other <u>two</u> * wives didn't -- but maybe you'll be the exception!

* [NOTE: ADJUST NUMBER OF "OTHER WIVES" ACCORDINGLY]

A ring symbolizes a lot of things ...

his love ...
his caring ...
his hopes for the future ...

[OPPOSITE PAGE]

Yeah! His hope he doesn't go bankrupt paying off that big-ass ring!

Bill & Sue -

You two are
so lucky!

Congrats on
finding
each other...

May you enjoy
your life
together!

before the
cops did!

- Larry

Congratulations on your engagement! I heard your
fiance' got you a really big exotic stone from a
foreign country -- funny thing, I've been looking on
my world map and I can't seem to find the country
of "Zirconia?"

Flo,

It's been said you can
tell a lot of things by
the size of the ring
he gives you...

If it's any smaller
than this: .

Dump him!

Don't worry, I'm not sending you one of those typical, silly "Greatest Father In The World!" cards. I think much more highly of you than to do that!

[OPPOSITE PAGE]

So, Happy Father's Day to the "Greatest Father In The <u>Universe!</u>"

Did I ever tell you that you remind me of a famous movie star?

[OPPOSITE PAGE]

Now can I borrow the car?

I just want you to know, although I never told you, as a kid I always looked up to you!

[OPPOSITE PAGE]

But don't get carried away -- I had no choice -- you were always taller than me.

Dear Dad,

Thanks, that one night anyway, for not using birth control!

[SIGNATURE]

[NOTE: MAY ALSO BE USED FOR <u>MOTHER'S DAY</u>*]*

Here's to the man who taught me just about everything I needed to know in life -- except about sex. But, then I learned about that the same way you did -- in the pool hall.

(We both know what "eight ball in the side pocket" really means   -- don't we!)

To the Dad who likes his beans ...

[OPPOSITE PAGE]

Happy Farter's Day!

Here's to the best Dad a person could have! You taught me everything I know: how to play baseball -- how to camp out -- how to be a man -- and when I have a kid of my own ...

how to punish him unmercifully!

(Just kidding -- you're the best!)

I always remember you the same ...

The bald head!
The baggy boxer shorts!
The beer belly!
Those foul morning farts ...

[OPPOSITE PAGE]

and the ability to take a joke!

Even the <u>very best</u> ain't good enough for you!

[OPPOSITE PAGE]

So I'm glad I got you something worth a lot less.

HERE'S TO A GREAT DAD!

Hey Pop -

Guess what?

I just got the news
that you're not
my real father!

(But I wouldn't worry - the lady
who told me that was not my
real mother)

Your son,

Joe

Sorry to hear you're going to be hospitalized for a while -- especially with medical costs as high as they are. But look at the positive side: at the end of your stay, they'll probably name the new wing <u>you</u> <u>paid</u> <u>for</u> after you.

Glad to hear your ___bypass *___ operation was a success!

Sorry to hear you only went in to remove a bunion!

* [NOTE: SUBSTITUTE APPROPRIATE MAJOR OPERATION]

You know, sometimes hospitals switch X-rays by mistake, but I wouldn't worry ...

And sometimes they give you someone else's medication, but I wouldn't worry ...

And every so often, during an operation, they take out the wrong organ, but like I said, I wouldn't worry ...

(I'd just get well and get the hell outta there as fast as possible!)

(FOR SOMEONE HAVING
AN EMOTIONAL SET-BACK)

I know things are a little tough right now, but do
you remember that old saying, "Let a smile be your
umbrella"? Well, don't try it! I did once and I got
water up my nose!

Sorry to hear about the operation!

I guess your Mom is going to have to cook up a
tanker-truck load of chicken soup to heal that one!

I realize it's pretty hard to do -- considering they're
feeding you "HOSPITAL FOOD" -- but get well soon!

Okay, so you've gained a little weight. So you're low
on money. And so you feel like all your friends have
deserted you ...

Look on the bright side:

More weight could keep you from being blown away
during a flash hurricane!

No money means you don't have to be worried
about being kidnapped and held for ransom!

And no friends means you won't receive dopey cards
like this which are meant to cheer you up, but don't!

Did you know that today's hospital food has been rated as being even worse than airplane food? Or that sanitary conditions in about 65% of our nation's medical facilities is now at an all-time low? And due to the recent rising number of malpractice suits, doctors are drastically cutting back on quality care?

(Sure took all the fun out of being deathly ill, didn't they?)

Remember the good old days when being in the hospital meant being slightly inconvenienced?

Now it means being slightly inconvenienced, moderately ignored, excessively drugged and completely broke!

(TO PERSON WITH LONG RECOVERY PERIOD)

Sorry to hear you're still not back to 100% !

But there's an upside to everything ...

[OPPOSITE PAGE]

You probably have the world's largest collection of sympathy cards!

Sorry about the cast!

Hope you get it off soon, so we can get it on!

Sorry to hear you're flat on your back!

(And I'm even sorrier that I'm not flat on your stomach!)

I want you to get well soon! So here's three things to think about that will speed things up:

1. A mean nurse
2. A large thermometer
3. Your butt

I hope you don't mind, but I've been having sexual thoughts about you while you've been in the hospital. I was picturing you dancing totally naked -- your supple breasts undulating up and down, your thighs pulsating to the music, your tight body slowly moving side to side -- but then I realized how weird this would look in that full body cast!

So get well soon!

Sorry to hear you're confined to a bed!

(But come to think of it, that's where you do everything best!)

Being in the hospital is <u>no</u> <u>laughing</u> <u>matter</u>!

(However, the thought of your butt on
that bedpan <u>is</u>!)

I'm so happy to hear that your hospital stay is over
and you are <u>fully</u> <u>recovered</u>! But from one
hypochondriac to another ...

I think you ought to get a second opinion!

Sorry to hear you're back in the hospital!

(But if you'd studied a little harder the first time,
you probably wouldn't have to take your urine test
over!)

Service at the press of a button ...

Breakfast, lunch and dinner in bed ...

Sexy nurses giving you sponge baths ...

And you want to go home???

[OPPOSITE PAGE]

What are you, <u>sick</u> ???

Just as I thought! Lying around in bed all day, as usual ...

(I always knew you were the type of person to let a little ___broken leg *___ slow you down!)

* *[NOTE: SUBSTITUTE APPROPRIATE <u>MAJOR</u> INJURY]*

Yo Mike!

I hope you don't mind, but I told the doctor that you really like

huge, razor-sharp hypodermic needles.

25 gallon boiling hot enemas.

and bland food!

but don't worry...

GET WELL SOON!

I don't think he believed me – about the bland food.

Your bud,

Nick

Congratulations on your graduation! And now, before you go out to face the world on your own, I want to leave you some words of wisdom ...

??? ... !!!

Darn! Where are those words of wisdom??? I could have sworn I had them right here!!!

Sorry, I must have left them in another card!

I want to give you some advice on the eve of your High School Graduation:

DON'T WASTE YOUR MONEY ON COLLEGE!

I didn't and look at me:

I'm my own boss! Nobody gives me orders! I don't have to punch a time clock! And I can go home whenever I want! Of course, I don't have a job, but that's beside the point.

[SIGNATURE]

P.S. Remember my motto: "Only a fool pays for skool!"

Dave

here am some impotent words of wisdum from someone whom, unlike yous, did not gradiate from collitch:

have self-estream!

Be chairful!

2ND

Keep Smelling!

—JohN

INTENTIONALLY POOR HANDWRITING

Well, it's time to do some deep and serious thinking about your future ...

[OPPOSITE PAGE]

So what do you want for breakfast, tomorrow morning?

The <u>best</u> is yet to come!

(Unfortunately, you have to go through about 25 or 30 <u>really</u> <u>crummy</u> <u>years</u> to get there!)

You are by far the sexiest, wildest, most erotic graduate in your class! I'm going to bestow a degree of my own on you ...

[OPPOSITE PAGE]

"Magna Cum Loudest"

Dear Alison,

Congratulations on your graduation!

You know, I never did graduate so there's something I've always wondered...

Is it true you're all buck-naked under those gowns?

Just Curious;

Doug

Congratulations on this very Special Day!

Congrats on your High School Graduation!

The good news is: in the Fall you're going to be starting college!

The bad news is:

[OPPOSITE PAGE]

You can't major in "Laying Out At The Beach And Drinking Beer While You Scan The Babes."

So, you struggled through four long years of college and finally got your degree.

Congratulations! You're now entitled to be a fully-credited waitress. *

* [NOTE: FOR MALE, SUBSTITUTE "WAITER"]

Well, it was a real struggle, but you finally got through school. Now you're <u>whole</u> <u>life</u> is ahead of you.

(Let's just hope you don't go through <u>it</u> with a "D" average, too!)

You know, some of us were betting you wouldn't
graduate. Now don't get us wrong, we're happy that
you did, but it cost us 2 houses, 3 cars and $50,000
in cash.

Jim,

Well it's time to
start thinking about
your future...

Can you spare a second?

Pops

I'm happy that you finally got your diploma, but I'm also surprised!

(I didn't think your principal * was the type to take a bribe!)

* [OR ... SUBSTITUTE REAL NAME -- e.g. "Principal Smith;" "Dean Johnson;" etc.]

[NOTE: THIS CAN BE USED FOR ALMOST ANY GIFT-GIVING SITUATION -- e.g. BIRTHDAY, XMAS, WEDDING, ETC.]

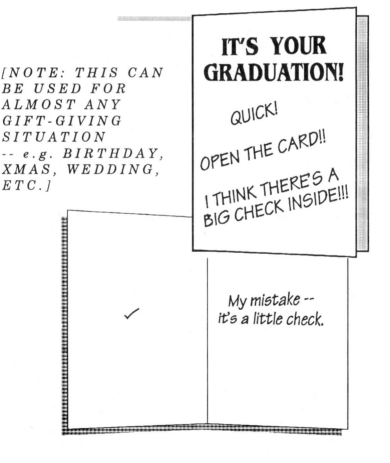

IT'S YOUR GRADUATION!

QUICK!

OPEN THE CARD!!

I THINK THERE'S A BIG CHECK INSIDE!!!

✓

My mistake -- it's a little check.

DAN—
WANT TO ATTEND
A COLLEGE WHERE YOU
WILL DEFINITELY GET
STRAIGHT A's ?
FILL OUT THE FOLLOWING
APPLICATION:

BEER GUZZLER U.
APPLICATION
1. Q: Do you like beer ?
   A: _____ *

* If "YES" – CONGRATULATIONS!
  You're on the Honor Roll!

—WOODY

CRUDELY DRAWN
APPLICATION:

It's Halloween, so I'm going to scare you -- and I'm going to do it with just <u>two</u> <u>little</u> <u>words</u>:

[OPPOSITE PAGE]

trust me!

Things to consider when choosing a mask:

1. It should not be made out of a toxic substance.
2. It should not be too obscure.
3. It should not look better than what's underneath!

BOO !   Did I scare you?   No, huh?   Let me try again: GRR !! Still didn't work, eh? Okay, I got a three-letter word that will for sure scare the crap out of you:

[OPPOSITE PAGE]

IRS !!!

Halloween is...

Painting up your face!
Putting on wild outfits!
And partying till ya drop!

Halloween is ...

[OPPOSITE PAGE]

Just a normal night for you.

Well, it's Halloween, so I'm thinking about "ghosts and goblins and THIGHS that go bump in the night!"

I have a suggestion for your costume this year:

dress up as a "Lady-of-the-evening!"

Why?

Because a trick from you would be a treat!

This year I'm going to wear the most frightening mask I can find. And maybe if I'm lucky ...

[OPPOSITE PAGE]

I'll scare the pants off you!

This year be sure to wear a real scary mask!!!

(It'll lessen the shock when you take it off!)

Well, I'm almost ready for Halloween:

I have the pumpkin carved, I have the costumes sewn, and some eerie music to play in the background. Now all I need is an ugly, scary, disgusting, pimply, monster face to put in my front window ...

so I was wondering if your Ex is available?

I usually like to wear something really scary, but this year, for my Halloween costume, I've decided to go for laughs!

(So can I borrow one of your suits?)

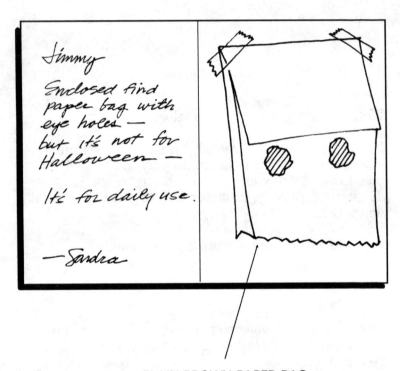

Jimmy

Enclosed find
paper bag with
eye holes —
but it's not for
Halloween —

It's for daily use.

—Sandra

PLAIN BROWN PAPER BAG
WITH EYE HOLES CUT OUT

HAVEN'T WRITTEN General

Sorry I seldom have time to write, but a rugged
sportsman like myself has certain obligations.
Summer is baseball season, so I'm busy whacking
home runs. Fall, it's the football field and I'm
putting bone-crunching tackles on half-backs.
Winter means the basketball court -- slam dunking!
And during the Spring I chase butterflies merrily
through fields of daffodils in my tutu.

Sorry I haven't written, but each month I have to
make my bills a priority. And by the time I finish
writing all those checks, my pen has run out of ink.

Here are my three favorite excuses why I haven't
written in such a long time:

[OPPOSITE PAGE]

1. I'm a schmuck!

2. I'm a schmuck!

3. I'm a schmuck!

Sorry you haven't gotten a letter from me for a while, but I've been having trouble turning my thoughts into words. So lately, I've been turning my words into thoughts -- and that's why I haven't written. But if it's any consolation, I have been <u>thinking</u> about you!

I know you don't want to hear another lame excuse of why I haven't written, but this time I have a very good one ...

[OPPOSITE PAGE]

I'm waiting for the price of ink to go down.

I could give you a dozen excuses why I haven't written -- but thank God you're a responsible and sensible person and wouldn't want to see me sit here for several more weeks trying to think of them!

I realize it's been a while since I've written, so to bring you up to date:

The good news is, I finally got my s--t together.

The bad news is, I can't get rid of the smell!

My Dear Sweet Tina,

I love you and I'm sorry I haven't written, but everytime I sit down to write you, I start fantasizing about how sexy you are and next thing I know -

REMEMBER ME?

my arm is too tired to write!

Love
Ted

I could give you a list of reasons why I haven't written that's as <u>long</u> as my arm -- or one reason that's as <u>short</u> as your .....

———

Over the past several months I've written a lot of letters to all my other friends and relatives -- and now I've finally gotten around to writing you.

(Would you believe me if I told you I saved the best for last?)

———

You would be well advised to put this card away in a safe place! (Because, by the time you get another one from me, it's bound to be a rare antiquity!)

IN CRAYON

Lori —
Sorry I aint wrote ya for a spell, but they're only just now lettin me have pointy objects here at Sunnyvale.

— Steve

Congratulations on your new job!

[OPPOSITE PAGE]

Now about that money you owe me ...

You deserve to be #1!

(But then there's me.)

So will you settle for second best?

Congratulations on owning your own business!

Of course, now <u>you're</u> the one who has to make payroll, buy company health insurance, pay all the bills, etc.!

But the good part is, for once you don't have to chip in on the boss's Christmas present!

We hear you're up for a promotion! That's great!
And to help you do your best when you go in for the
final "interview" we all are going to chip in and buy
you a pair of knee pads!

Congratulations!

I heard that as a little bonus, to go along with your
promotion, you're going to get off a little earlier!

(I don't know, sounds like a "nooner" to me!)

Congrats on your new job!

You know, work is a lot like foreplay!

(You try real hard -- you sweat a lot -- and in the
end, you get screwed!)

Congrats on the promotion! *

I'm sure that, at first, things'll be confusing and complicated and you'll feel like you don't fit in.

But, I'll bet, in no time at all, you'll get the hang of being totally incompetent!

* [OR -- on becoming the new manager!]

Congratulations on another promotion! Since I know how ambitious, conscientious, and dedicated a worker you are, all I can say is ... looks like you fooled 'em again!

Congratulations! Now that you're starting your new, executive job, one piece of advice: lose the Roy Rogers lunch bucket!

Perry, ol' buddy -

Don't worry about that promotion - it's in the bag!

I had a talk with the boss about how you're a real asset to the company!

GOOD LUCK!

(I told him that all those office supplies you made off with over the years were 100% deductible!)

Your Pal,

Fred

Darling, for you I promise to give up <u>drinking</u>, <u>partying</u>, and my <u>wild</u> <u>sexual</u> <u>fantasies</u>!

No, wait! I promise to give up <u>drinking</u> and <u>partying</u>!!

No, wait! I promise to give up <u>drinking</u>!!!

No, wait! ... Okay, I got it! I promise to give up <u>making</u> <u>promises</u> I can't keep!!!!

You want sex? You want eroticism? You want juicy, lascivious, arousing dialogue? You want steamy, luscious panting and cooing?

How about a sexy erotic voice telling you they're longing to fulfill your wildest fantasies? Well, now there's a number you can call to get all this <u>and</u> <u>more</u>!

[OPPOSITE PAGE]

Mine: _____

    [YOUR NUMBER]

[NOTE: ALSO WORKS AS A BIRTHDAY OR CHRISTMAS CARD:

For your birthday, do you want sex? Do you want eroticism? Do you want ...]

(TO NEW GIRLFRIEND) *

Honey, my love is pure and natural -- no flavor
enhancers -- no emulsifiers -- no nitrates, nitrites,
sodium bisulfate, BHT or other chemical additives --
and thank God, since I left my wife, my love is also
<u>fat</u> <u>free</u>!

* *[NOTE: THIS CAN BE SWITCHED TO
(NEW BOYFRIEND)]:*

... since I left my <u>husband</u> ...]

(TO NEW LOVER)

If you show me yours, I'll show you mine!

(But unfortunately, <u>mine's</u> being fixed.)

[OPPOSITE PAGE]

My <u>car</u> of course -- what did you think I was talking
about?

(TO NEW LOVER)

Yesterday morning, <u>before</u> <u>getting</u> <u>out</u> <u>of</u> <u>bed</u>, I called my Mom and wished her "Happy Birthday." I then wrote out a large check to the Humane Society. And finally, I composed a short speech to the U.N. expressing my views on World Peace. I did all this while <u>still in</u> <u>the</u> <u>sack</u>!

(You see, I just wanted to prove to you that I am <u>good</u> in bed.)

You're such a hunk! I'm really turned on by your bulging muscles, your hairy chest, your tight buns! But my favorite part of you is your throbbing, gigantic ...

[OPPOSITE PAGE]

heart.

I'm kind of thinking about maybe considering the possible idea of perhaps inviting you to hopefully come by for something sort of like maybe a little drink, if that's okay with you? Huh???

(But I'm a little worried you might think I'm too aggressive!)

I want you to touch my body in a lot of foreign places!

(Paris! Rome! London!)

I'm really <u>working on</u> that "sensitive" thing
New-Age men are suppose to be.

[OPPOSITE PAGE]

(But until I get it down -- let's screw!)

I'll bet you're wondering what I'm feeling after last
night ...

Nothing from the waist down!

I may not be a magic Genie, but, tonight in bed, if
you rub me three times, I'll make your next "wish"
come true!

You know, it's always been hard for me to say to you
I L...

I L... I L...

[OPPOSITE PAGE]

I Like To Get Laid!

Just for the heck of it, let's say that your sex organ is called an "end". And mine is also called an "end". The reason I bring this up is ... I'm trying to make ends meet!

Darling, you're everything I ever wanted in a woman ... beauty, charm, poise, sensuality, wit, intelligence ...

(and your hooters ain't bad either!)

Heather,

Sigh! Pant! Pant! Oh, I could make you happy! Do you want me to tell you what I could do? Sigh! Pant! Pant! Well, I could lick your ... No, no, better yet, I could bite your ... Oh! Oh! I'm getting so turned on I can't stand it anymore! Sigh! Pant! Pant!

Love Franz,

P.S. Sorry for sending this card, but my phone was out of order.

Sometimes, after an exciting evening with a man, I feel like giving him a hand ...   in your case, I feel like giving the finger!

After our last date, all I can say is, some people's minds work wonders ...   with you, it's a wonder your mind works!

Last night inspired me to write a poem:

Roses are red,
And violets are blue.
Sugar is sweet,
Screw you!

Before our date, I thought you were a <u>friend</u>!

(Now I think you are an <u>enema</u>!)

When I first met you, I wanted to spoil you rotten!

(But now it's starting to smell like I'm too late.)

(GIRLFRIEND TO GIRLFRIEND)

Did you hear that I lost some dead weight?

<u>210 lbs</u>. * to be exact!

I did it on the _____ diet!

  [YOUR EX'S NAME]

* *[SUBSTITUTE THE WEIGHT OF YOUR EX-BOYFRIEND]*

Wendy,

Hi. sex How are you doing? sex
I am sex fine. I sex thought you
might like to sex go out to dinner,
sex sometime? And sex then maybe
a movie sex afterward? And you
sex thought I only sex had one
thing on my sex mind!

Love!

Bart

I miss you and I really need to see you soon because I'm starting to have trouble remembering what you look like!

This morning I tried to picture you in my mind and all I got was a TV test pattern!

Just thought you should know -- I'm <u>naked</u> as I write this card!

(Because I can't <u>bare</u> to be without you!)

Did you hear the big news???

"HELL JUST FROZE OVER!"

So, now can we try it again?

I've been thinking about you <u>very</u> <u>hard</u> -- and that's what it's getting me!

I hope you return soon. You know I love you and wouldn't want to ever hurt you -- but I'm starting to think about asking my hand for my own hand in marriage!

That's right, grab it with your left hand, squeeze tight and bring it up to your mouth. Now open wide and get ready -- but first, take your right index finger, gently probe until you find a hole. Insert it and ...

[OPPOSITE PAGE]

Dial my number -- talk to me -- I miss you!

It's hard to say where I would be <u>without</u> you ...

but if I was <u>with</u> you ...

we would be in bed!

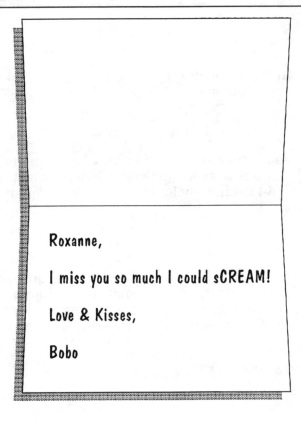

Roxanne,

I miss you so much I could sCREAM!

Love & Kisses,

Bobo

Whenever you are away, I can't <u>tell</u> you how hard it is ...

(But when you come back, I'll <u>show</u> you!)

When I think of you, I think of:

Inspiration!
Fascination!
Stimulation!
Captivation!
Delectation!
Palpitation!
Titillation!
And most of all:
Penetration!

Can't wait to see you!

I love you!
I miss you!
I need you!
And <u>on</u> <u>top</u> of everything else,
I'd like you <u>on</u> <u>top</u> of me!

I know what you're doing is important, but I wish
you'd hurry up and come home. Not only because I
miss you, but for health reasons ...

(My right hand is beginning to cramp up on me!)

I can't tell you how much I miss you!

[OPPOSITE PAGE]

Because I <u>don't</u>!

I think it's so flattering when someone misses you, don't you?

which gives me an idea ...

[OPPOSITE PAGE]

How about if you go away?

I've spent days, weeks, months trying to think of a way to describe how I miss you! (I couldn't think of a thing, but time sure flew by!)

IN INK

Maureen—
I get so excited
thinking about you
that I

INK BLOB

Sorry, premature
Ink-ulation!

— Randy

IN PENCIL

I think you're getting better every year ... at accepting the fact ... that from me ...

[OPPOSITE PAGE]

you're only getting a card.

[NOTE: ALSO FATHER'S DAY]

(FROM HUSBAND--OR <u>ONLY</u> SON/DAUGHTER)

Today is a very special day! It's <u>your</u> day! The celebration of you being a <u>mother</u>!

And I'm as proud as can be that <u>I'm</u> personally responsible for making you one!

(FROM A SON WHO IS ENGAGED)

This is a "Dear Mom" letter:

I don't know how to tell you this, but I have found someone else to cook, sew and clean up after me. It looks pretty serious, this time, but just in case, please don't rent out my room!

(LARGE FAMILY)

Although there were a lot of us in our family, I've always felt that I was your favorite child. And now I have a confession:

(You were my favorite Mom!)

Happy Mother's Day to "The Greatest Mom In The World!"

(All of us kids took a vote and it was unanimous!)

Of course, there are a lot of other Moms in the world, but I promise ...

[OPPOSITE PAGE]

you're my one and only!

You are the kindest, most thoughtful and caring person I have ever met. You always have been there for me when I needed someone. You have supported me when I was uncertain, encouraged me when I was doubtful and cheered me on when I was winning. No matter what, you have always made me feel important -- which brings me to this question ... are you for real?

This may not stand up in court, but I have to confess ...

[OPPOSITE PAGE]

as a Mother, you're "Exhibit A!"

I love shopping for <u>shoes</u> at I Magnin!

And I love picking out <u>blouses</u> at Bloomingdales!

But I love you the most, Mom ...

[OPPOSITE PAGE]

because you are where I got my <u>genes</u>!

I love you because you have always been there for me!

As a teenager, you were a shoulder to lean on.

As a youngster, you were a shoulder to cry on.

And when I was a baby, you were a shoulder to throw up on!

To the wonderful Mom who brought me into the world ...

Though now I'm out on my own, living in my own apartment, I must confess -- sometimes I miss my old <u>womb</u>!

A
MOTHER'S DAY
MESSAGE!

Mom,

It's always been difficult
to talk about sex with you,
but here goes...

He slowly caressed my ~~back~~
Our lips met passionately and ~~~~
We could wait no longer so ~~we made~~

Oh well, I gues some things
never change. Meanwhile,
Happy Mother's Day!

Karen

Hey Mom, don't have a cow!

[OPPOSITE PAGE]

Have a happy M-udders Day!

I decided to give you this card instead of flowers ...

[OPPOSITE PAGE]

It's a real pisser trying to write "Happy Mother's Day" on a petunia!

I owe a lot to you, Mom! Thanks to you I grew up with self-respect, a sense of pride and honor. I often ask myself, where would I be without you ...

(Probably stapled between the pages of a girly magazine!)

I know it was always difficult to talk about "the birds and the bees" ...

but now that I'm married, I have to ask you a question ...

[OPPOSITE PAGE]

What do you do if he only has a 2 inch "stinger?"

[AUTHOR'S NOTE: Of course there's <u>nothing</u> *on this page -- the last thing* <u>we</u> *would ever condone is someone insulting their Mother!]*

They say "a woman's work is never done" -- and beings it's Mother's Day -- and beings I'm your loving daughter -- I'm going to help out!

(I'm buying you a new mop.)

Dear Mom,

You always tried to teach me to be practical. That's why I'm giving you a card instead of a "Mother's Day Bouquet" ...

Flowers will die in a couple weeks and you'll have to throw them out. This card, you can keep forever!

You were always a wonderful Mother to all of your children!

Your hard work, your dedication, your sacrifice has been a real inspiration to me ...

[OPPOSITE PAGE]

I'm never having kids!

Mom,

You're more than just a
Mother to me! You're someone
I can BANK on! Whenever
you're not arround, I have
WITHDRAWALS! And even
though I can't always
ACCOUNT for my (trans)
ACTIONS, remember you're
never aLOAN -- you'll always
have me to SPEND time with!

Well, I'm gonna go to my room
now and listen to some CD's.

Enough hints!
Can I borrow some money?

Sincerely,

Corey

Dear Mom,

Happy
Mothers

Day!

fRom THE SoN
WHo's RooM
WAS
ALways
A MeSS!
LoVe
Bill

Well, once again it's time to throw a wild party, get plastered and make a big fuss over New Year's. But it's starting to make very little sense??? I mean, if New Year's is suppose to represent a "<u>new</u> start," how come we always begin it with an <u>old</u>-fashioned hang-over?

Will you be having another wild party this year?

I hope so, because last year I was so drunk, I can't remember if I had a good time!

I think I figured out why most people get drunk on New Year's Eve ...

It's a great excuse to forget all those stupid, impossible resolutions you made.

It's the New Year! Time to be daring and try new things!

(So next year, when we have sex, how about if I get to be on top?)

You know how most people break their New Year's resolutions practically the next day? Well, this year I'm going to make some resolutions I know I can keep!

"During the next year I resolve to ...

[OPPOSITE PAGE]

1. get older!

2. get fatter!

3. lose more hair! and

4. fart uncontrollably when company's over!"

Sweetie --

If you bring the champagne, come midnight ...

[OPPOSITE PAGE]

I promise I'll pop your cork!

There are some people who only use New Year's as another excuse to <u>get</u> <u>drunk</u>.

But I know you better than that!

(You use it as another excuse to <u>stay</u> <u>drunk</u>!)

Dearest Sam,

Well, it's time to break out the booze and get drunk out of our minds...

because at midnight, we're going to have to kiss an ugly bunch of relatives and friends!

    Your loving wife,
    Eve

Happy New Year!

HAPPY NEW YEAR!

Mark,

Okay, so here's my resolution:
I resolve to write you ...
~~everyday~~
~~once a week~~
~~twice a month~~
~~every other year~~
~~next decade~~
a nice eulogy.

Your friend,

John

Don't I know you? Weren't you a person who <u>used to</u> write me?

Or are you just a figment of my aggravation?

This is your final notice!

If you don't write me, you're out of my will !!!

[OPPOSITE PAGE]

Okay, that's a little harsh, you can stay in my will, regardless. But if you don't write me, I'm going to outlive you!

(PARENT TO YOUNG SON OR DAUGHTER)

I don't want to sound like a complainer, but I'd like to hear from you sometime -- you don't have to rush, but hopefully before I'm a <u>grandmother</u> and you're making the same complaint!

PLEASE WRITE

R-Rated

I just thought of something long and thick you could wrap your hands around and put your mouth up to...

[OPPOSITE PAGE]

(a telephone -- call me!)

You know, if you had sex as often as you write letters...

[OPPOSITE PAGE]

you'd still be a virgin!

I know you're not as good as I am with keeping up correspondence, but if you don't pick up a pen <u>soon</u> and tell me you love me ...

someone else will be "flicking my Bic!"

It's been so long since I've seen you I can't remember your face ...

[OPPOSITE PAGE]

Unfortunately, your breath is always with me!

Lost your pen?

No stationery?

Out of stamps?

Can't think of anything new to say?

[OPPOSITE PAGE]

Or are you just sparing me the dreary details of an incredibly boring life?

I know you're mad at me for the things I said. But I didn't mean to hurt your feelings -- it was just the heat of the moment. You must know I didn't truly mean what I said! So can you please find it in your heart to forgive me? Okay? Pretty please?

[OPPOSITE PAGE]

Thanks, you stupid jerk!

(TO KID AT COLLEGE)

Well, you're off to college and you're very busy,
what with getting an education and all, but I know
in my heart that you will pick up this letter and
respond, some day, <u>soon</u> ...

[OPPOSITE PAGE]

like, as <u>soon</u> as you need money!

Dear Santa,

Please write!

Sincerely,

Paula

*P.S. Of course I know you're
not Santa. But I figure my
chances of getting a response
from him are better than
from you!*

[ENCLOSE]:

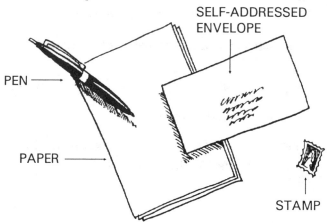

[ATTACH POST-IT NOTE]:

Now what's your excuse?

(TO SOMEONE LIVING FAR AWAY -- ESPECIALLY IN A REMOTE AREA)

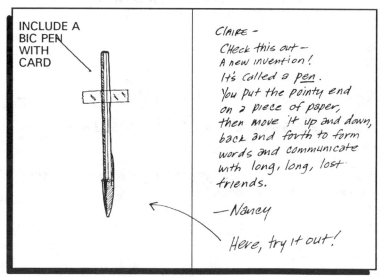

Congratulations on getting out of the Rat Race!

Now let's just hope you saved up enough cheese!

Congratulations on your retirement!

And just remember this: you're not too <u>old</u> to do your job -- you're too <u>young</u> to spend the rest of your life working!

Here's hoping your retirement is rich and rewarding!

(<u>Unless you've made other arrangements</u>?)

[NOTE: THIS PUNCH LINE WILL WORK FOR ALMOST ANY HOLIDAY:]

Here's hoping you have a terrific Mother's Day! (unless ...

Have a happy Valentine's Day! (unless ...

Hope you have a wonderful Christmas! (unless ...

May you get exactly what you want on your birthday! (unless ...

ETC.

According to top psychologists, sex is supposed to be better after you retire!

[OPPOSITE PAGE]

Now if you can just remember how it's done ...

I understand you're considering retirement. Just think ...

No more unrealistic deadlines!

No more putting up with employee negligence!!

No more taking orders from incompetent superiors!!!

No more chasing the opposite sex around the office????

Wait a minute -- are you sure you want out?????

There's no reason sex after retirement can't be just as exciting as when you were a teenager!

[OPPOSITE PAGE]

Providing you find white hair, wrinkles and shriveled up sex-organs a real turn on!

Retirement is a time to reflect upon all you've accomplished over the years ...

So think about it a minute, then open another beer and sit back down in front of the TV!

Well, you've reached that ripe old age where it's about time to start thinking about a high-fiber diet, drinking a lot of prune juice and contemplating that move to Florida for your health ...

(Then again, you could just save your money and get a cemetery plot.)

It's been a joy working beside you all these years! I have a lot of fond memories!

(The days you were off sick and your vacations especially come to mind!)

The best years of your life are still ahead of you ...

[OPPOSITE PAGE]

Too bad you're too old to enjoy them.

―――――――――――

Now that you are no longer working, you probably have planned all kinds of fun activities ...

[OPPOSITE PAGE]

The Intravenous 500!

Hemorrhoid Tossing!

And Bed Sore Trivia!

―――――――――――

(BOSS TO EMPLOYEE)

I was happy to hear you finally decided to retire! I'm not saying you were getting too old, but I was afraid someone at work was going to trip over your oxygen hose and sue us.

(GROUP CARD)

To William:

After years and years
of working with you,
the thought of you
leaving brings a tear
to our eyes. We're
all so sad to see
you go. We'll miss
your sense of humor
- the funny jokes you
told in the break room -
that reassuring smile
as you walked past
our desks every
morning.

You never failed
to lift our spirits!
So, there's one
thing we've got
to know before
you leave...

What exactly was
your job here?

- the Gang

Rob Chuck MONA
Don Paul Rabecca
Gene Inez Nina

Happy "National-Excuse-To-Eat-Like-A-Fat-Pig"
Day!

It's time to celebrate the Thanksgiving traditions
established by our ancestors many years ago when
the Pilgrims would gather together to give solemn
thanks for the harvest, partake in a sumptuous
feast, then turn on the football game and guzzle
beer.

(TO LOVER/HUSBAND/WIFE/
BOY-OR-GIRLFRIEND)

Okay, I admit it. Lately I've been inconsiderate and
somewhat insensitive to your feelings. But look at it
on the bright side: this Thanksgiving you're getting
<u>two</u> turkeys!

It's Thanksgiving -- time to eat a turkey.

(But enough about your sex life!)

Rod—
In keeping with the tradition of Thanksgiving...

I'm giving you the bird.

—Denise

CRUDE ILLUSTRATION OF HAND
WITH MIDDLE FINGER EXTENDED

It's Thanksgiving, the day we eat turkey -- which in your case is known as cannibalism!

HAPPY THANKSGIVING!

Vern -

The answer:

"A 42 lb. Tom, or You!

and

the QUESTION IS....

"What's the biggest turkey on record?"

Your Bro, Earl

HAPPY GREETINGS® $1.95

(TO A VEGETARIAN)

Your Invited!

You are cordially invited to a <u>vegetarian</u>
Thanksgiving dinner.

(I promise the turkey we're
preparing <u>never</u> ate meat!)

I don't know how I can ever thank you for your warmth, concern and that special <u>personal</u> <u>touch</u> you add to everything you do!

(But if you think of something, have your people get in touch with my people!)

I want to take this opportunity to thank you for being such a special friend! I don't know what I would have done without you. Whenever I have needed a <u>real</u> friend you have always been there for me! I just can't thank you enou... wait a minute ... don't you owe me ten bucks? And from over a year ago?? C'mon you sleazy low-life, fork it over!   Hey, just kidding, pal! (I think it's really only <u>five</u> bucks.)

You have given my life very special meaning! And now I want to give you something that will brighten up your day and make you feel better than you've ever felt ...

[OPPOSITE PAGE]

a McDonald's "Happy Meal"

I don't know how I can ever pay you back ...

But if you think of something that includes whips, leather and handcuffs, give me a buzz!

Tomorrow morning I'm sure I'll be thanking you for <u>nothing</u>!

(If tonight that's what you're <u>wearing</u>!)

Thanks to your outrageous, disgusting and perverted sexual fantasies, I've been sore for three days!

[OPPOSITE PAGE]

So are you free again next weekend?

Whenever I receive a gift from you I'm never disappointed ...

[OPPOSITE PAGE]

I just keep reminding myself, "It's the <u>thought</u> that counts, It's the <u>thought</u> that counts ..."

I want to thank you for the lovely gift. It was just about almost very close to precisely not quite exactly what I wanted!

You have been very helpful to me and I really wanted to pay you back ...

(Unfortunately, I needed the meter money.)

What a wonderful gift! You must have put a lot of thought into it! What excellent taste you have! By the way, you didn't happen to save the receipt, did you?

(Just kidding--it's perfect!)

I want to thank you for the gift! It's terrific! It's one of the best gifts I've ever received! Perfect color, too! You have such good taste ... wait a minute ... it was you who bought me the Corvette, right?

I was up all night, last night, trying to think of a way to thank you ...

so I didn't get a bit of sleep, I'm going to be late for work, and they'll probably fire me when I get there...

Thanks a lot!

Nothing would give me more pleasure than to shake your hand in person!

But since I can't be there, grip this card in your right hand and move it heartily up and down!

[OPPOSITE PAGE]

and hope no one caught you doing this!

Lately I've been undressing you with my eyes -- and it's been real exciting -- except for these button marks all over my face!

Preparation H?

Lemons??

Motor oil???

Vapo-rub?????

Liverwurst?????

Broccoli????????

Cat litter????????

Fish guts??????????????

OPPOSITE PAGE]

I just can't think of anything sweeter than you!!!!!!

I just wanted to let you know that I love you for your mind!

(Of course, the rest of the package ain't bad either!)

Happy Valentine's Day, Sweetheart!

Because I had some <u>very</u> <u>special</u> feelings for you this morning, I drew a red heart, wrote your name on it, then cut it out and pinned it to my lapel.

So Darling, today I have a "heart on" for you!

You know, lately I've been thinking that I'd like to see you in a different <u>light</u> ...

[OPPOSITE PAGE]

like, hanging naked from my <u>chandelier</u>!

How do I love thee? Let me count the ways ...

[OPPOSITE PAGE]

1. with you on top

2. me on top

3. doggie style

4. 69 position

5. in the shower

6. outdoors

7. with sex toys

[CONTINUE UNTIL YOU RUN OUT OF ROOM ON THE CARD]

(MAN TO WOMAN)

There's a couple of things about you that make me love you more than ever ...

[OPPOSITE PAGE]

Your right one and your left one.

Nothing turns me on like you do!

(Well, if you don't count that one dream I had about the ten sex-starved pygmy women.)

This is a special X-rated card ...

[OPPOSITE PAGE]

INSTRUCTIONS:

Open and close this card several times -- slowly at first -- now faster, faster! Harder, harder! -- scream out "Oh Baby! Oh Baby!!" -- then smoke a cigarette.

Dear Valentine,

My heart aches for you!

It is a burning pain I can't describe ...

BURP!

Hmm ... that's better ...

My mistake -- it must-a been that chili I ate.

You remind me of the cute, little puppy that followed me home one day ...

[OPPOSITE PAGE]

It turned into a mean 'ol dog!

Roses are red,

And violets are blue.

Sugar is sweet,

And a new nose would look good on you!

WITH A PENCIL, PUNCH "BULLET HOLES" ON THE INSIDE
BACK COVER OF THE CARD ONLY, SO THEY AREN'T SEEN
UNTIL THE CARD IS OPENED

[ON OUTSIDE OF CARD]

[ON INSIDE OF CARD:]

(2ND / 3RD / 4TH / ... / MARRIAGE) *

Congratulations on your ___third *___ marriage! Don't worry that the others didn't work out -- think positive:

[OPPOSITE PAGE]

"Practice makes perfect!"

What a rigorous day today must have been! The tension of the ceremony, the 6+ hour reception that never seemed to end, the long drive to the honeymoon suite! Well here you are at last and I bet you can't wait to pop open a bottle of champagne, jump on the heart-shaped bed and start ripping ...

[OPPOSITE PAGE]

open these envelopes and counting that money!

This is just a card to celebrate your wedding.

(It's not a lot, but at least it isn't another Cuisinart!)

Congratulations on your wedding! Now, remember that on your wedding night in your honeymoon suite, you're going to have to do exactly what your husband wants. So be prepared:

bring plenty of beer and make sure the TV has the All-Sports Channel!

Here's how it works:

In the church, you tie-the-knot.

At the reception, you tie-one-on.

In the honeymoon suite, you tie-each-other-up.

Any questions?

———

May every wonder of marriage, you never miss,
May you often look back and think of this,
May her love always be as strong as his,
May you never be too tired to kiss,
May each other you never ever dismiss,
May your caring be a bottomless abyss,
May all your life be filled with bliss,
May ... I be excused, I have to piss!

———

Here's something to keep in mind when you are
saying your vows:

[OPPOSITE PAGE]

In about three or four hours you will be doing it
doggie-style!

(TO A COUPLE "EXPECTING")

Not only are you two the perfect <u>wedding</u> couple, you're also the perfect <u>beach</u> couple:

You're great at lying around doing nothing and your wife provides ample shade!

(GIRLFRIEND TO GIRLFRIEND)

Wishing you Love and Happiness!

Tanya,
Congratulations! Now if you just spend as much <u>nighttime</u> with your husband in bed as you spend <u>daytime</u> with your girlfriends in malls, it should last forever!

Love, Lisa & Kim

Oops! I just found out the caterer got the Bachelor Party and the Wedding Reception instructions mixed up ...

Keep your fingers crossed that the <u>naked</u> <u>babe</u> doesn't pop out of your wedding cake!

You're a couple with a lot of class!

I'm really looking forward to an exceptionally chic wedding and, of course, an elegant reception!

(I just hope you don't run out of hot dogs and baked beans too early in the evening!)

(FOR: YOM KIPPUR, ROSH HASHANAH, HANUKKAH, ETC.)

MAZEL TOV!

DAVID -

HAPPY "HARD-TO-SPELL" JEWISH HOLIDAY!

LOVE,

Greta

JOHN CARFI has been a stand-up comedian for over 13 years. He started at The Comedy Store in L.A. and now makes his home on the East Coast. He has opened for the rock group Styx, Belinda Carlisle, George Carlin, Tony Bennett and many others including his personal favorite, The Teenage Mutant Ninja Turtles. John is currently a radio personality on the popular "Keith and John Morning Show" (WZZO 95.1 FM in Allentown, PA.) Although his show begins at 5:30 a.m., he sets his clock to 5:30 <u>P.M.</u> just so he feels better about getting up.

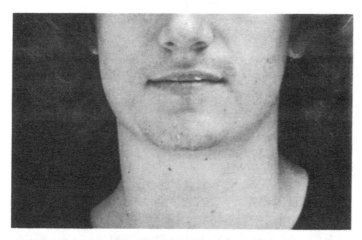

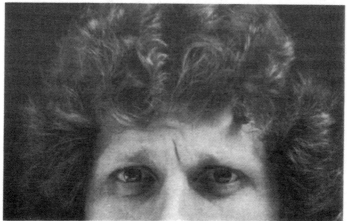

CLIFF CARLE has been a comedy writer all his life (stand-up comedy, comedy revues, comedy sketches, Sit-Coms, comedy this, comedy that). He has co-written (with John Carfi) six comedy books, plus seven comedy cassettes including the NO HANG-UPS series (Funny Answering Machine Messages) which have sold over a million copies worldwide. His one regret in life is no one takes him seriously.

TITLES BY
CCC PUBLICATIONS

— NEW BOOKS —

NEVER A DULL CARD [$5.95]

WORK SUCKS! [$5.95]

THE UGLY TRUTH ABOUT MEN [$5.95]

IT'S BETTER TO BE OVER THE HILL — THAN UNDER IT [$5.95]

THE PEOPLE WATCHER'S FIELD GUIDE [$5.95]

THE GUILT BAG [$6.95]
(Accessory Item)

HOW TO **REALLY** PARTY!!! [$5.95]

THE ABSOLUTE **LAST CHANCE** DIET BOOK [$5.95]

HUSBANDS FROM HELL [$5.95]

HORMONES FROM HELL [$5.95]
(The Ultimate *Women's* Humor Book!)

FOR **MEN** ONLY [$5.95]
(How To Survive Marriage)

THE Unofficial WOMEN'S DIVORCE GUIDE [$5.95]

HOW TO TALK YOUR WAY OUT OF A TRAFFIC TICKET [$4.95]

WHAT DO WE DO NOW?? [$4.95]
(The Complete Guide For All New Parents)

— COMING SOON —

THE BOTTOM HALF

LIFE'S MOST EMBARRASING MOMENTS

HOW TO ENTERTAIN PEOPLE YOU HATE

THE KNOW-IT-ALL HANDBOOK

— BEST SELLERS —

NO HANG-UPS [$3.95]
(Funny Answering Machine Messages)

NO HANG-UPS II [$3.95]

NO HANG-UPS III [$3.95]

GETTING EVEN WITH THE ANSWERING
MACHINE [$3.95]

THE SUPERIOR PERSON'S GUIDE TO EVERYDAY
IRRITATIONS [$4.95]

YOUR GUIDE TO CORPORATE SURVIVAL [$4.95]

GIFTING RIGHT [$4.95]
(How To Give A Great Gift On Any Budget!)

HOW TO GET EVEN WITH YOUR EXes [$3.95]

HOW TO SUCCEED IN SINGLES BARS [$3.95]

TOTALLY OUTRAGEOUS BUMPER-SNICKERS [$2.95]

THE "MAGIC BOOKMARK" BOOK COVER [$2.95]
(Accessory Item)

— CASSETTES —

NO HANG-UPS TAPES [$4.98]

(Funny, Pre-recorded Answering Machine Messages With
 Hilarious *Sound Effects*) — In Male or Female Voices

Vol I: GENERAL MESSAGES

Vol II: BUSINESS MESSAGES

Vol III: 'R' RATED MESSAGES

Vol IV: SOUND EFFECTS ONLY

Vol V: CELEBRI-TEASE (Celebrity Impersonations)

Bonus!

Template

IF YOU WANT TO

"CREATE YOUR OWN CARDS"

JUST...

1. CUT OUT

2. XEROX SEVERAL COPIES

3. CUT TO SIZE AND
   FOLD IN HALF

4. PICK A MESSAGE FROM
   THIS BOOK AND LET
   YOUR IMAGINATION
   GO WILD!

CUT HERE

---------- FOLD ----------